SISTERS

ISBN 0-7624-1790-0

Quotes have been abridged and adapted
from the original work, *Sisters.*

Cover and interior design by Serrin Bodmer
Edited by Jennifer Kasius
Typography: Centaur MT and Shelley Andante Script

This book may be ordered by mail from the publisher.
Please include $2.50 for postage and handling.
But try your bookstore first!

Running Press Book Publishers
125 South Twenty-second Street
Philadelphia, Pennsylvania 19103-4399

Visit us on the web!
www.runningpress.com

SISTERS

Reflections on the Unbreakable Bond

A Journal

by Carol Saline & Sharon J. Wohlmuth

RUNNING PRESS

PHILADELPHIA · LONDON

*M*y sister is my barometer.
I can tell her things I can't tell anybody else.

We used to be close because we had to be . . . .

Now we're close because we want to be.

We need each other like we need light and air.

When I think about who I am attached to

or who is most important to me, it is my sister.

I've learned a whole lot about life from my big sister,
for which I will always be grateful.

I can't imagine what it would be like not to have a sister to support me, to tell me the truth, to be there for me—whatever it is I need.

*F*rom birth to death, sisters delight in each other's happiness and comfort each other's tears.

My sister is an
eternal presence who
warms my heart and soul
and shares my memories.

The older you are, the more you need your sister.

Sisters are your role models—
they teach you how to become a woman.

My sister, myself.

The ties that bind sisters are fierce, fragile, and forever.

Sisters respect each other's strengths
and laugh at each other's weaknesses.

*W*e get a kick out of the same things;
we will laugh at stuff nobody else finds funny.

My sister makes the world a safer place.

*M*y sister is the person who shows me what I want from others.
She sets the standard everybody else has to match.

Without using words, we just know things about
each other. There is tremendous security in that.

Whatever happens in my life,

I will never be alone because I have a sister.

My sisters have shaped me into the person I am today.

*Nobody can love you like a sister
and nobody can hurt you more.*

There's this feeling that if your sisters won't accept you for who you are, then who will?

I would feel empty without my sister.

I trust her with my life.

My sister is the part of myself that talks back.
She is so much like me, but also different.

*S*isters are like an immutable law of
the universe that nothing can destroy.

The beautiful part of a sister's friendship is knowing she will never go away.

Our sisters hold up our mirrors; our images of who we are and who we can dare to become.

My y sister has shown me different ways to grow—
I'm grateful to her for always being there.

*I*t doesn't matter that we have different interests or lifestyles . . .
we've learned to love each other, and we'll never stop.

*No matter what—my sisters are there.
There's no choice—we'll always be related.*

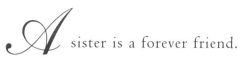

A sister is a forever friend.

As we get older,
we no longer have to
be the big sister or the
little sister . . . we
can just be girlfriends.

Your sister is the only one who knows exactly what you mean when you talk about your mother.

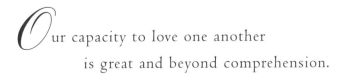

*O*ur capacity to love one another
is great and beyond comprehension.

*L*ife is truly most rich when you can
share a textured past with your sisters.

Within a family, sisters are often the most competitive with one another. But once they grow up, they have, by far, the strongest relationship.

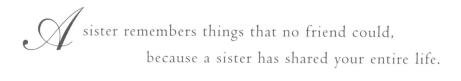 *A* sister remembers things that no friend could,
because a sister has shared your entire life.

My sisters and I know which buttons to push to set one another off. But out of respect, we don't push them. There's never a reason to hurt your sister. Never was; never will be.

Over the years we have
built a bond that connects
us like patches in a quilt.
It's sewn together so perfect
and neat, this relationship
where it's safe to retreat.

*M*y sisters:
Without you, I am but
one corner of life,
one piece of a puzzle,
one side of a conversation.
    With you, I am whole.

*S*isters learn to celebrate their differences and
appreciate one another for their individualism.

*W*hen one sister needs help,

the others are her support system.

*O*ur lives and interests are not at all alike, but we
have a strong sense of unity and security that grows
from the love that holds us together.

My sister offers me laughter and forgetting.
I'm careful to never take our relationship for granted.

My sister deserves a medal for all
her courage, her love, and her selflessness.

By destiny joined, intervention divine,
forever and ever our hearts entwined.
That's my link to this sister of mine.

*I*t's very hard in this life to find someone who can walk a mile
in your shoes; a sister comes closer to that than anyone else.

My sister and I are so different that it's hard to imagine we are related, let alone that we could be so close.

The key to a good sister relationship is balance.
Neither sister feels she gives more than she gets in return.

I never have to explain myself
to my sisters. They recognize exactly
where I'm coming from because
they've been with me along the way.

We have brothers we love, but there's no comparison with our relationship. For them, the primary women in their lives are their wives. For us, it's each other.

No one in your life can aggravate
or disappoint you more than your sister.
And no one can love you more, either.

*L*ucky me!
My sister picked a husband
who isn't bothered by our need to
talk to each other five times a day.

*T*he key to a good sister relationship is not to expect
more from a sister than you would from a good friend.

I can leave so many things unsaid with my sister
because I'm already so familiar with her.
I know what shaped her personality. We have the same history.

*S*isters not only share a stock of memories;
they speak the same household language.

What I can offer my sister is a sanctuary,

a safe haven.

I know she would do the same for me. That's what sisters are for.

I have only one sister and she is the
only sister I would want to have.

*The most special and rarest gift in life is
having a wonderful sister.*

*Nobody has the ability to make me feel
as good about myself as my big sister.*

*O*ur motto is: "We don't like each other all the time, but we always love each other."

I look forward to our matching rockers

on the porch of our future.

My sister and I are bonded through past and parents.

You can have all the friends in the world, but your dearest and truest friend will always be your sister.

ear sister,

You are always in my thoughts and never far from my mind
and soul, even though we are separated by three thousand miles.
Thankfully, we can share our joys and stresses on the telephone.

I'm glad you are my sister;

I'm blessed you are my friend.

My sisters have always been my comfort zone. Now with daughters of my own, I know the richness of what they have together because I've experienced it myself.

*S*isters have a private language
they speak without words.

My sister is a woman, separate from my mother
and my daughter, who challenges me and yes,
angers me but most importantly, understands me.

*W*hat a joy it is to have a sister at the other end of the phone line to talk with, laugh with and offer support when we need it.

When my sister and I became adults,

we started to relate outside the context of family.

We realized then that we weren't just sisters, we were really pals.

What could be more amazing than sisters who live one thousand miles apart, yet buy the same clothes, read the same books and feel the same feelings?